THE SPICI

Kateryn the Qwene KP

THE SPICE OF WISDOM

Praying with Katherine Parr

John Partington

KENELM PRESS

First Printing, March 2013

ISBN 978-0-9575927-0-4

Published by Kenelm Press

www.kenelmpress.co.uk

Printed in the United Kingdom

CONTENTS

Mario Testino ©

I was delighted to visit Sudeley Castle again last year as Patron of the Queen Katherine Parr Quincentenary Festival. It was a particular pleasure to be shown a copy of Katherine Parr's Prayer Book in the library and later, led by John Partington, to spend a few quiet minutes near her tomb in St. Mary's Church saying together some of the prayers written by Katherine herself.

Few women's writings have come down to us from so many centuries ago. In the pages that follow are found not only some of the carefully crafted prayers that Katherine intended for publication, but also the more personal hopes and fears of a woman who was as passionate in her faith as she was in other aspects of her eventful life.

In this new translation John Partington hopes to bring Katherine Parr's writing to a wider audience. Her voice speaks to us still: her commitment to what is right and good, expressed with humility and openness to others, is as valuable now as it was in the more turbulent times of the Tudors.

Camilla

HRH The Duchess of Cornwall

INTRODUCTION

Many know of Katherine Parr only as the last wife of
Henry VIII – the one who 'survived'. Some will also know
that as the stepmother of Henry's children (especially of the
future monarchs Edward VI and Elizabeth I) she had a significant influence on the future development of the monarchy
and therefore of England itself. But of the woman herself,
many will have only a hazy awareness.

Katherine had a striking personality and varied talents: she
was passionate, intelligent and cultured. She was also a
woman of profound spirituality in an age of religious ferment.
Converted to a reformed understanding of, and a deep personal faith in, God's grace in Christ, she was a leading proponent
of the protestant faith in the court of Henry VIII, and had a
significant influence on the reforming zeal of the young
Edward VI.

At the same time, however, she had an instinct for reconciliation – clearly apparent in her prayer 'In Time of War'
(page 21). This desire for harmony meant that throughout her
life she found sustenance not only in a dependence on God's
grace as taught by the Reformers, but also in the devotional
writings of more traditional, 'Catholic', authors. In her
personal, unpublished, book of prayers (page 29) she included
both strands of spiritual writing, Catholic and Protestant, and
even seems at times deliberately to have alternated them. In
so doing she marked out a harmonizing form of the Christian

religion which found its flowering many years after her death, in the Church of England that emerged in the reign of her stepdaughter Elizabeth.

Katherine Parr was buried in St Mary's, Sudeley in what is now the parish of Winchcombe in Gloucestershire (the only queen to be buried in an ordinary parish church). I was instituted as Vicar there on the anniversary of her death, and chose as my prayer at that service part of her prayer of self-offering (page 16), words that have since become a regular part of our parish's commemoration of her life.

Last year we celebrated the 500th anniversary of Katherine's birth. I know that it would have pleased her that as part of our commemoration we set up a charitable fund in her name for the benefit of local young people. I think it might also have intrigued her that another royal consort kindly agreed to be Patron of the year's celebrations – Her Royal Highness the Duchess of Cornwall, who shared in our praying some of Katherine's prayers at Sudeley during the year, and who has generously written a short foreword for this book.

John Partington
February 2013

In the following pages I have translated Katherine's words into a more modern idiom, quite freely on occasion but at all times seeking to communicate the essential meaning of her writing. Any inelegance of phrasing is almost certain to be mine rather than hers.

PRAYERS FOR EVERY DAY

These prayers are taken from Katherine's second book, Prayers or Meditations, *published in 1545. It was a work of great originality, and even of daring, being the first work in English to be published by a woman under her own name, and being written at a time of bitter religious controversy, when to be accused of heresy (as Katherine was on at least one occasion) could lead to death. In another sense, though, the work is not entirely original, being a shortened, and rewritten, version of Richard Whitford's 1532 book* The Following of Christ, *itself a translation of Thomas à Kempis' Imitatio Christi. Katherine's rewriting, however, breathes new, reformed, life into the work and in the process puts into words a spirituality that still resonates today.*

God's wisdom   Without you, Lord, no pleasure lasts for long. If anything is to stop life tasting so bland, it must come from you – for your wisdom is the true spice of life.

Lord forgive me, because when I pray I find it hard to concentrate on you. Often, it's as if I'm not really there, wherever I'm standing or sitting, but somewhere else, where my thoughts have taken me. So I am where my thoughts are – and where my thoughts are most often, that reveals what's most important to me. What comes into my mind most frequently are the things that I find greatest pleasure in and those that I prefer to think about. Lord, you yourself said in the Gospel, "Where our treasure is, there will our heart be". So let me, unworthy as I am, find pleasure only in you, and not in myself nor in anything else except you.

I want to find true contentment in you, Lord, but I can't manage it. I want to be consistently spiritual, but lesser concerns keep dragging me down. There's a battle going on inside me, and it's painful: part of me wants what's right and good, and part of me wants the opposite. It really hurts. I try to concentrate on spiritual things, and straight-away a great rabble of worldly thoughts rush into my head. So, Lord, don't leave me alone for long; don't give up on me. Send the fiery heat of your love to burn away the cloudy fantasies of my mind. And then, Lord, reassemble my thoughts ... in you.

Lord, give me inner strength. Help me to understand that all things in this life are transitory, so that I may not waste time worrying about them, nor be led astray by placing too much importance on them. They, like me, will pass away – for nothing under the sun lasts long: it's all emptiness, and trouble, in the end. Instead, Lord, give me your wisdom from above, so that in learning to put you first I may enjoy your presence and, above all, I may love you.

Lord Jesus, help me never to set my heart upon worldly things, but instead may all superficial attachments (to things in the world around or to things within myself) fade away. May I find my security in you – no longer restless, and with my heart content. For you, Lord, are the heart's true peace and the soul's true rest, and without you everything brings fretfulness and stress.

for a right perspective

Lord, I want to confess to you all my shortcomings, and the unstableness of my heart. Often something quite small becomes a big problem for me, and stops me wanting to live for you. And sometimes I'm full of good intentions, but then something quite minor throws me right off balance. Lord, you can see my weakness; you know my frailty better than anyone. Forgive me, and rescue me from everything that's wrong with me, so that I don't become trapped in it. Help me to rest in you, and to find peace in you, more than in anything else – more than in others' opinions of me, more than in any worldly status, more than in my own schemes, more than in health or good looks, more than in being wealthy, more than in human pleasures, more than in being well thought of, more than in any worldly happiness except what I find in you. For you, Lord God, are the best, the wisest, the highest, the mightiest, the most sufficient, the most full of goodness, the sweetest, the most comforting, the most attractive, the most loving, the noblest, the most glorious – the one in whom all goodness most perfectly is. So whatever I have besides you is nothing to me: for my heart finds no rest or peace except in you.

Lord, I'm glad that I'm nothing special in human terms, in which case other people's praise might lead me astray. I know that no-one should be ashamed or discontent at being ordinary or not well-off, but rather should be grateful for it. You yourself chose insignificant people, looked down upon by others, to be your servants and close friends. In the same way, Lord, please help me to find as much satisfaction in being the least as others find in being the greatest, to be equally content to be in the lowest place as in the highest, and to be as glad to be unknown as others are to be important or famous.

Lord, those who please themselves without you, displease you; and those who take delight in the praise of others lose the praise that really matters – yours. True praise is to be praised by you, and true happiness is to find happiness in you. So may your name, Lord, and not mine, be praised; may what you do, rather than what I do, be well thought of; and may it always be your goodness, not mine, that is well spoken of. You are my true glory, and you are the one who gives me real happiness. So help me to find glory and happiness in you, and not in myself nor in any worldly status: compared to your eternal glory, those are a shadow, mere nothing.

self-
offering

Lord, you know what is most profitable, and most suitable, for me. So give me what you want, as much as you want, and when you want. Do with me what you want – in whatever way pleases you and is most to your glory. Put me wherever you wish, and do with me whatever you please. You made me, and I am in your hands: so lead me in whichever direction you want. Lord, I am your servant, fully at your disposal: my desire is not to live for myself, but for you.

God's will
to be our
will

Lord Jesus, may I always want, and may I always intend, whatever is most pleasing to you. May what you want be what I want – and may what I want be always to do what you want. So may my intentions and desires always be the same as yours; and may I never wish for anything less, nor anything other, than to do your will.

Lord Jesus, your decisions are good, and what you want for me is better than anything that I could plan or even imagine for myself. So do with me whatever you want, for everything you do is only ever for the best. Whether you want me to be in light or in darkness, I bless you for it. If my life is comfortable, I bless you for it – but if I find trouble rather than comfort, I bless you for that too. Give me the grace, Lord, to accept gladly whatever shape my life takes, and patiently to receive from you things both good and bad, bitter and sweet, happy and sad. So help me, Lord, in whatever circumstance, to thank you for it.

Lord, you know that I'm not good at coping with things, and that it doesn't take much to bring me low: strengthen me with your Spirit so that I may be able to endure all sorts of trouble for your sake.

when others let us down

Lord, help me in my trouble, for others' help is of little use. How often have I been disappointed, when I looked to someone else for friendship? And how often have I found it where I least expected? It's a waste of time trusting in other people: what really works is to trust in you. So I bless you, Lord, in whatever happens to me, for I am weak and unstable, easily deceived and quickly changing. Lord God, most righteous Judge, strong and patient, you know people's weakness and their ill-intent: may you yourself be my whole strength and comfort when trouble comes, for I can't trust my own judgement.

for God's comfort at all times

Jesus, Lord of my life, please be with me always and everywhere. When I have no worldly comfort may I find a special solace in you – and if at any time I lose touch with even your comfort, keep me from despairing and help me patiently to wait for whatever you intend next for me.

Jesus, King of Glory, you bring joy and comfort to all Christian people in their wanderings as pilgrims in the wilderness of life. My heart cries to you in quiet longing, and my silence speaks to you, saying "How long will my Lord God delay in coming to me?". Lord, come to me: for without you I have no real happiness, and without you my soul is heavy and sad. It's as if I'm in prison, shackled by sadness, until you, Lord, come to me in your loving kindness, bringing me joy and freedom of spirit, and blessing me with your presence. So open my heart, Lord, to know what you want and to do it, and help me to remember how much good you have done to me, so that I may thank you.

Lord Jesus, closer to me than any human lover, where can I find wings of perfect love, to fly from my earthbound sadness and find my rest in you? When will I rise above my present state to see, and feel, your love for me? When will I be so absorbed in you, that I'm no longer aware of myself, or of things around me ... but of you, above all things? When will you be as real to me as you are to those who truly love you?

God's true wisdom

Lord, show me how to do what you want – to live humbly and worthily before you. For you are my true wisdom; you know me as I really am; you knew me before the world was made, or before I was born into it. To you, O Lord, be honour, glory and praise for ever and ever. Amen.

A PRAYER IN TIME OF WAR

In the summer of 1544 Henry VIII left England to pursue a military campaign in France, appointing his new queen, Katherine, as regent of the realm in his absence. It was probably at that time that she composed this prayer, "for men to say, entering into battle".

The prayer is striking in its lack of triumphalism, in its shrinking from bloodshed and in its desire for reconciliation. It comes to us across the centuries as an example of how we might pray for peace in our own troubled times.

Almighty King, the true Commander of armies, peace and war are both under your control.

David was small, unarmed and without military training, but you gave him the courage and strength to attack and to overcome with a sling-shot the huge giant Goliath.

We believe that our cause is just, and that this battle has to be fought: we beg you therefore, Lord God, to turn our enemies' hearts to desire peace, so that no human blood may be spilt.

If not, then grant, Lord, for your glory's sake, that with little bloodshed and with small hurt or damage to those not involved, we may obtain victory.

May the war soon be ended and our differences resolved, so that we may all find unity and common purpose in praising you – who live and reign for eternity.

Amen.

THE LORD'S PRAYER

While most of her prayers were composed by reworking others'
material, it seems likely that the following meditation, which
Katherine entitled "A devout prayer, daily to be said", was entirely
her own work. Its sections follow, and amplify, the biddings of the
Lord's Prayer.

Almighty and eternal God, you have made it possible for
each one of us, like a heavenly child, to call you our
heavenly Father: grant that your most holy name may be
honoured among us by the evident purity and innocence of
our lives. So may those around us, seeing the good things
that you do in and through us, be moved to give glory to
you.

Lord, may the kingdom of your grace and mercy reign
continually in our hearts, so that we may be worthy of a
share in that place where glory and majesty are to be
found. May we, till the day we die, do what you, Lord
God, want – following the example of those whose home
is in heaven, as we never resist that most holy will but
rather obey it without disagreeing with one another, united
in spirit, laying aside controversy, overcoming human
desires and all worldly and spiritual temptations.

Give us food for our bodies, Lord, so that we may more
effectively live for you. Give us also, we pray, the
heavenly bread – the body of your son Jesus Christ, the
food that brings wholeness to our lives. Give us the bread

of your commandments, so that we may shape our lives upon them. And give us the bread of your heavenly word, which fortifies us inwardly, so that we may be well fed and at the end prove worthy to join the heavenly feast where all hunger ends.

Lord, may we not be overwhelmed by temptation, and lose our way because of it. Instead, in all the danger that it brings, when its storms beset us, may we your children be aware of your fatherly help, so that we're not overcome by the deceits of the tempter that lead to our destruction. Instead, may temptation's fire test and refine us, so that at the end, having lived whole-heartedly for you, we may be with you for ever in that heavenly city against which no temptation can prevail.

Finally, most merciful Father, we pray that through your kindness and goodness we may be rescued from all bodily and spiritual evil both now and in the time to come. May we at the last, free from all that oppresses us in this life, inherit the kingdom won for us, your children, by your Son who died for us. May we find there, for ever, the fulfilment of heavenly delight with the whole company of heaven, through the kindness and help of our Saviour Jesus Christ. To him with you, our Father, and the Holy Spirit, be glory and honour, now and for ever.

Amen.

GOD'S WISDOM

Katherine's first publication, dating from the year before her Prayers or Meditations, *was an anonymous translation of Thomas Fisher's 1525* Psalmi seu Precationes, *('Psalms or Prayers'). The work consisted of fifteen 'Psalms', which were in fact a recasting of material from throughout the Old Testament writings. The passage below is an excerpt from her translation of Fisher's fifth Psalm, 'For the Obtaining of Godly Wisdom', and includes verses not only from the Psalter, but also from the books of Wisdom, Daniel, 1 Chronicles and Proverbs.*

Lord God of mercy, who by your word have made all things, and by your wisdom have created humankind;

Eternal God, to whom everything is known, however secret it may be; you who know everything before it takes place:

Open my lips and my mouth, so that I may speak and declare the glory and praise of your name.

Give me a new heart and a right spirit, and take from me all wicked and sinful desires.

Lord, I am foolish, ignorant and blind when I lack the knowledge that comes from you ...

Please give me, your servant, a teachable heart so that I may always know what pleases you.

Send down from heaven the spirit of your wisdom, and refill my heart with knowledge of it ...

With you, Lord, are riches, glory and righteousness – treasures which will never fade.

Whoever finds you finds life, and whoever does not love you loves death ...

When you have taught me your wisdom I shall speak out and declare your praise and glory.

Then I will proclaim your wonders, so that others too may turn to you,

And may bless your name for ever, to the end of time. Amen.

THE END OF SIN

Published shortly after the death of Henry VIII, Katherine Parr's 'Lamentation of a Sinner' was a strikingly humble account of a sinful life transformed through faith in God's grace in Christ – a book so self-abasing that Sir William Cecil, a member of the Privy Council, devoted his preface to an appeal to readers to receive it charitably as an example of the honest repentance necessary for all who would receive Christ's forgiveness.

After some closely-argued pages written in a personal style, Katherine broadens her reference to 'all of us' in her closing paragraphs:

I wish that all of us, when circumstances suggest, might admit our shortcomings openly ... But, sadly, we're so fond of ourselves that we're unaware of our own faults. And if ever we do notice our own guilt, we either put a favourable gloss upon it, or we're ashamed to admit it at all. What's more, we take offence at, and are hurt by, anyone pointing out our faults even in a loving and godly way: we fail to distinguish between loving advice and malicious accusation. Surely, if we really cared about God's glory as we should, we wouldn't be ashamed to admit that we wander from his ways, since it's obvious that we do – and indeed that we do so every day?

I pray that what we've done wrong will not condemn us at the end of time, when all of us will reap the consequence of our actions ...

When that day comes, we shall have no defence lawyer to plead our case, nor can we have our case deferred. The just Judge will not be swayed by personal considerations, nor by a bribe; he won't hear of any excuse or delay; nor will any saint or martyr help us, however holy they are. Ignorance won't save us from condemnation – though wilful blindness and obstinate ignorance will receive a greater punishment, and rightly so.

At that time it will be made clear who has 'walked in darkness', for everything will be laid open before God. No-one's deeds will be hidden, nor their words and thoughts. Poor and simple keepers of God's commandments will be rewarded with everlasting life, as obedient children of their heavenly Father. But those who break God's law, and those who add to it or subtract from it, will justly be condemned.

My prayer is that we shall escape that fearful verdict, and that we shall be found to be such faithful servants and loving children that we may hear the happy, comforting and most joyful verdict, destined for God's children: "Come here, you who are blessed by my father, and receive the kingdom of heaven, prepared for you from before the beginning of the world".

To the Father, the Son and the Holy Spirit be all honour and glory, world without end.

Amen.

FINAL PRAYERS

When Lady Jane Grey went to the scaffold in 1553 she took with her a little manuscript book of prayers. It has only recently been realized that that small volume had in fact been written, and passed to her, by Katherine Parr. Although, like most of Katherine's other compilations of prayers, it was composed largely of translations and reworkings of others' writings, it is in fact a most remarkable document.

What is so striking about this collection of prayers, which was probably never intended for publication, is the careful way in which it combines traditional ('Catholic') and Reformed prayers, even deliberately alternating them at times. Although theological disagreement divided western churches in the sixteenth century, Katherine preserved and presented a devotional unity between them – a unity which found expression in the English Church which emerged after her death.

Two of the prayers in Katherine's final, and most personal, prayer book were translated from a collection written by the traditionalist Thomas More during his imprisonment in the Tower of London before being executed.

r help in
trouble
Lord, give me patience in my troubles, and grace in everything to conform my will to yours, so that I may truly say "Your will be fulfilled on earth, as it is in heaven". The things, good Lord, that I pray for, give me grace to work for.

*for our
enemies*

Almighty God, have mercy upon me and upon all those who show me ill will and who would do me harm. In your infinite wisdom and kindness pour out your gentle, tender, merciful mercy on their faults and mine, so that all wrong may be righted and we may be brought safely together to heaven. There, for the sake of our dear Saviour who himself suffered sorely, may we live and love together for ever with your blessed saints and with you yourself, our threefold God.

In keeping with her reconciling intent, Katherine follows More's two prayers with two by the reformer Nicholas Shaxton, originally published on the title page of Miles Coverdale's 1535 translation of the Bible. The second of them was based on part of Psalm 119:

*when
reading
the Bible*

Lead me, Lord, in your way, and let me walk in your truth. May my heart rejoice in honouring your name. Shape my life according to your word, so that no wickedness may hold sway in me. Help me to walk in your paths, and keep my feet from turning away in the wrong direction.

*After many pages of longer and more formal prayers, the book
concludes with five shorter petitions of a more urgent nature, based
on Richard Taverner's translation of a prayer book by Wolfgang
Capito, an associate of Luther. Katherine entitled the first two
'A Prayer in Trouble' and 'For the Lightening of the Holy Ghost':*

*when sad
or in
trouble*
Lord, hear my prayer and have compassion on me.
Turn my sorrow into joy. Take this sadness off me
and clothe me instead with joy, so that I may give
you glory and praise you continually. Lord God,
rescue me from this trouble, and I will sing your
praise for ever.

*when in
pain*
Lord Jesus, I'm hurting. Hear me when I cry to
you for help. When you're with me I have nothing
to be afraid of; when I'm in trouble you bring me
joy and you comfort me by your Spirit. Pour upon
me your grace, and answer my prayers. May the
light of your face shine upon me, Lord: and as you
look kindly on me, may I be aware of you through
your Spirit, and so find lasting happiness. Lord,
you can do everything: give me peace, firm hope
and faith in you for ever.

Katherine's writing becomes fainter and more of a scrawl. Her final prayer is unfinished:

> Lord, you love me so much. I've put all my hope and trust in you. Don't let go of me ... Rescue me and help me ...

Katherine Parr died on 5 September 1548 at Sudeley Castle in Gloucestershire.

Her funeral, two days later, was the first to be conducted in the English language and paved the way for the following year's 'Book of Common Prayer'. Her tomb is still to be seen in St Mary's Church in Sudeley.

AFTERWORD

Katherine's prayers, excerpted and paraphrased in this small book, give us more than just a glimpse of a personal spiritual journey; they also open a window on a time of extraordinary development in the English church and nation. Her writings do not simply reflect the theological ferment of the time – they also helped to shape it.

A copy of *Psalms or Prayers* (page 25) now in the collection at Elton Hall in Cambridgeshire contains some fascinating notes written in the margins by King Henry VIII and Princess (later Queen) Elizabeth.

Henry's notes take us right to the heart of a Reformation debate – that about penitence. Opposite the printed phrase "I have not done penance" he has written

True repentance is the best penance.

and later in the book, alongside the words "... promised frequent forgiveness to those who do penance", he has written '*Remember best penance*'. At its outset, Henry's break with Rome may have had more to do with his matrimonial ambitions than his theological opinions – but here we see in his own handwriting the effect that Katherine's protestant understanding had begun to have upon him in his later years.

Princess Elizabeth's notes, in Latin, are equally remarkable. Strikingly, they are written in the name of Katherine Parr and her final husband Thomas Seymour – being signed with their names, and in their style.

The first is a reflection, perhaps prompted by Katherine's death in childbirth:

> *Death may be the way into future immortality ... but it's an absolutely horrible physical experience.* [a]

        The note is signed "Queen Katherine" and even includes the series of linked loops that Katherine herself used (as in the signature reproduced as a frontispiece to this booklet).

The second note is alongside the printed text "Beyond doubt, from my earliest days I have conducted myself proudly". In Elizabeth's distinctive handwriting is written:

> *Vanity of vanities, and the height of vanity.* [b]

        Not only is this signed with the name of Thomas Seymour (executed for treason in 1549), but it mischievously includes the monogram TR – 'King Thomas'.

---

[a]   "Mors est ingressus quidam immortalis future, quæ tamen est maxime horribilis carne. Catharina Regina R."

[b]   "Vanitas vanitatum et summa vanitatis"

The third note is again ostensibly by Katherine, and again with a copy of her signature:

We should distance ourselves firmly from the opinions of those who judge happiness by what is expedient in this life. The wholeness we should seek is not something that the world can offer, but is the gift of Christ to those who belong to him. [c]

Ten years were to elapse between Katherine's death and the accession of Elizabeth to the throne – a decade in which the life of the nation swung from radical Protestantism to reactionary Catholicism. But in the age of the first Elizabeth, to which England and its church owe something of their nature to this day, we find echoes of the spirituality of Katherine Parr, royal wife and stepmother ... and advocate of a pragmatic, inclusive Christian faith.

---

[c] "Debemus longissime abesse a sententia eorum qui metiuntur felicitatem commodis huius vitæ. Salus optanda est non quam mundus det, sed quam Christi suis largitur."

DATES IN KATHERINE'S LIFE

1509   *Henry VIII accedes to the throne*

1512   born to Thomas & Maud Parr (August)

1529   marries Sir Edward Burgh (or Borough)

It was probably during this first marriage that Catherine was converted to a Reformed faith in Christ

1533   widowed for the first time

1534   marries John Neville, third Baron Latimer

1536   *Pilgrimage of Grace*

a revolt against Henry's ecclesiastical reforms, in which Latimer was implicated and suspected as a result of treason

1543   widowed for the second time (March)

marries King Henry VIII (July)

1544   publishes 'Psalms or Prayers'

Queen Regent of England (July - September)

during Henry's absence in France

1545   publishes 'Prayers or Meditations'

1547   widowed for the third time (January)

On Henry's death, his only son (and Katherine's stepson) Edward acceded to the throne, and a period of significant church reform was begun.

publishes 'Lamentations of a Sinner'

marries Thomas Seymour (May)

1548   moves to Sudeley Castle

daughter Mary born (August 30)

dies (September 5)

1549   Thomas Seymour executed (Mar)

Book of Common Prayer published

ACKNOWLEDGEMENTS

This book would have been a great deal more difficult to write without the scholarly, and wise, work of Dr Janel Mueller in her '*Katherine Parr: Complete Works & Correspondence*' (Chicago 2012). In that, and in a number of shorter works, Dr Mueller has expertly drawn out both Katherine's reformed emphases in her translation work and her significance as a female writer in a male-dominated age. I'm grateful for her personal encouragement in my production of this booklet,

The family and staff at Sudeley Castle have been tirelessly supportive of my efforts – both in allowing access to historical material and in offering advice. Lady Ashcombe and her archivist Jean Bray deserve special thanks for their help in these regards.

Finally, my wife Elisabeth and my family more generally – not least my mother-in-law Mary Brettell – have offered support and advice in equal measure. I have taken grateful advantage of all of the former and of most of the latter.